A New True Book

PENGUINS

By Emilie U. Lepthien

This "true book" was prepared
under the direction of
Illa Podendorf,
formerly with the Laboratory School,
University of Chicago

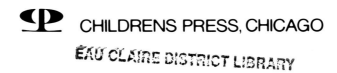

CHILDRENS PRESS, CHICAGO

King penguins

PHOTO CREDITS

Emilie Lepthien—cover, 2, 7 (right), 8 (top) 11, 15, 17,19 (right), 22, 25, 27 (right), 29 (2 photos), 30, 33, 35, 36, 37, 39, 41, 42 (2 photos), 44 (top)

Mark Rosenthal—7 (left), 8 (bottom right), 10, 12 (2 photos), 19 (left), 21 (2 photos), 27 (left), 44 (bottom)

James P. Rowan—20 (2 photos)

John Forsberg—4

COVER—King penguins

To good friends—Vivian, Marjorie, Marge, Alice, Erna, and the late Rosalyn Lasky

With appreciation for the advice from
Dr. George Llano, who has served with the National Science Foundation
  and the Smithsonian Institution
Dr. Frank Todd, Corporate Curator of Birds, Sea World, San Diego, California
Dr. Arnold Small, Harbor College, Los Angeles, California and the
  captain, staff, and crew of the *M.S. World Discoverer*

Library of Congress Cataloging in Publication Data

Lepthien, Emilie Utteg.
  Penguins

  (A New true book)
  Includes index.
  Summary: Describes the habits, behavior and life cycle of a number of the seventeen species of penguins, which in nature are found only south of the equator.
    1. Penguins—Juvenile literature. [1. Penguins]
I. Title.
QL696.S473L46   1983   598.4'41   82-17911
ISBN 0-516-01683-0   AACR2

15 16 17 R 02 01 00 99 98

TABLE OF CONTENTS

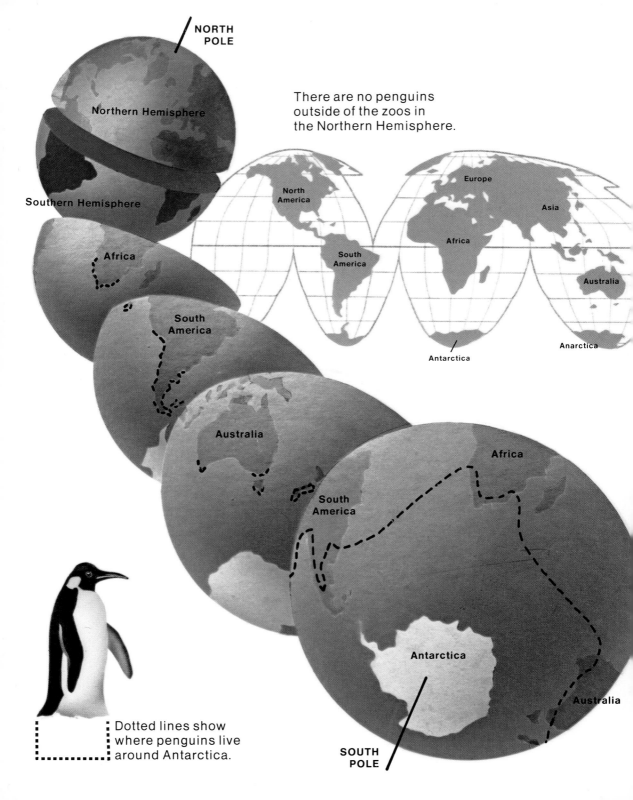

NORTH POLE

Northern Hemisphere

There are no penguins outside of the zoos in the Northern Hemisphere.

Southern Hemisphere

Africa

South America

Australia

Europe

Asia

North America

Africa

South America

Australia

Antarctica

Anarctica

South America

Africa

Australia

South America

Antarctica

Australia

SOUTH POLE

Dotted lines show where penguins live around Antarctica.

PENGUINS ARE SPECIAL

Penguins are very special birds. They have wings, but they cannot fly. They are expert swimmers, but they seldom use their webbed feet to paddle. Usually they mate for life.

Penguins return year after year to the same rookery. Penguins even return to the nest they used the year before.

Penguins have white breast feathers and black head, back, and flipper feathers. Only a few kinds have some colored feathers. There are seventeen different kinds of penguins.

Except for those in zoos, no penguins live north of the Equator. Penguins live in the southern part of the world. Four kinds of penguins live in the icy waters of the Antarctic. Only two, however, the emperor and the Adélie, can live south of the Antarctic Circle.

King penguin

Adult Adélie penguin

Gentoo penguins
with their babies

Feathers
normally
lay flat

Feathers
ruffle when
skin is hot

Magellanic penguins

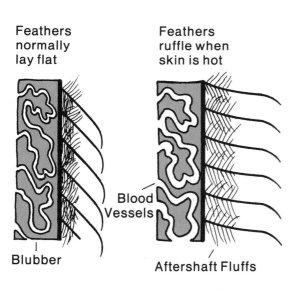

Blood
Vessels

Blubber

Aftershaft Fluffs

When penguins get too
hot their feathers ruffle
and the blood vessels in
the blubber swell to allow
heat to escape.

PENGUINS ARE ALIKE IN MANY WAYS

Penguins all have a thick layer of special overlapping feathers. Under their skin there is a layer of blubber or fat. This keeps them warm.

To cool off they pant or hold their flippers away from their bodies. They also fluff up their feathers.

Humboldt penguin

All penguins use their flipper-wings to swim. They use their feet and tail to steer themselves.

Penguins must come up to breathe. They leap up out of the water to take a quick gulp of air.

Penguins find all of their food in the sea. They eat small fish, squid, and krill. Krill look like small shrimp.

Baby penguins must be fed by their parents. The parents gather food in the sea. The food is partly digested by the adults. This is called "regurgitation."

Adélie penguin feeding its chick. Baby penguins are called chicks.

Fairy penguin

King penguins

PENGUINS DIFFER IN MANY WAYS

Penguins differ in size and weight. The smallest penguin, the little blue fairy, stands only 16 inches (40.6 cm.) tall. The emperors are the largest. They may be 45 inches (114.3 cm.) high. Smaller kinds of penguins live where it is warmer. The larger penguins generally live where it is colder.

13

In the Antarctic the female emperor lays one egg in May or June. It is dark twenty-four hours a day then.

The mother bird passes the egg to her mate's feet. He will hold it there for almost nine weeks. A flap of skin like a feather blanket will keep it warm.

Rockhoppers sitting on their eggs. Can you find the one newly hatched chick?

The mother birds will go out to sea to feed. They return just in time for the eggs to hatch. Then it is the males' turn to eat.

In December, summer returns to Antarctica. The emperor chicks will have grown or developed their warm, waterproof suits. They will be ready to go out to sea to feed themselves.

The female king penguin lays only one egg, too. The male holds the egg on his feet.

King penguins in molting stage

Kings mate on beaches
free of ice and snow. Most
king rookeries are in the
sub-Antarctic, often where
there is tall grass.

Crested penguins live on islands south of Australia and New Zealand and on the Falkland Islands off Argentina. Some go to islands in the sub-Antarctic. The six kinds of crested penguins are rockhopper, macaroni, royal, fiordland-crested, erect-crested, and snares-crested.

Crested penguins have yellow bristles that stick up on their heads. They may nest on grasses or the rocky ground. The female lays two eggs.

Left: Rockhopper Penguins
Below: Rockhopper with her two eggs

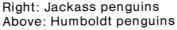

Right: Jackass penguins
Above: Humboldt penguins

There are four striped penguins. The jackass or black-footed penguin lives off southern and southwestern Africa. The Humboldt nests on the coast of Peru and Chile.

Above: Galapagos penguins
Left: Magellanic penguins

The Magellanic is found in southern Chile, Argentina, and on the Falkland Islands. The Galapagos penguins live the farthest north. They live along the shores of the Galapagos Islands at the equator.

21

The smallest penguins are the little blue or fairy penguins. They weigh only 2½ pounds (1.1 kg.). Their nests are in burrows. Here they are safe from hunting birds. The burrows also keep them cooler.

Other penguins, such as the Magellanic penguin (below), also live in burrows.

Fairy penguins have no defense against enemies ashore. For this reason, they spend the day at sea and return at night.

Yellow-eyed penguins nest in southern New Zealand and islands farther south. They, too, dig burrows or build their nests under the roots of trees or shrubs.

BRUSH-TAIL PENGUINS

On some islands off the Antarctic Peninsula the nests of all three "brush-tails" can be found near each other. Each kind—the Adélie, the gentoo, and the chinstrap—has its own territory.

All "brush-tails" spend most of their time at sea. For months they swim north of the Antarctic where they have their colonies or rookeries.

Chinstrap rookery. Penguins come back to the same place year after year.

By September and October the penguins begin the long trip back. It is spring in the Antarctic. The penguins will have only a few months to mate and raise their chicks.

Scientists study penguin habits by attaching numbered bands to the flippers of pairs of birds. In this way they learn that the same birds return to the rookery year after year.

Penguins come ashore to mate. They do not mate until they are at least four years old.

First the male or father birds return. They start the long walk over ice and snow to reach the old rookery. Their short, stubby legs make walking difficult.

Left: Adélie penguin in a zoo
Below: Gentoo penguin on snow

At last the male Adélies reach their old nests. They must get busy immediately collecting pebbles. The pebble nest is important. It will keep the eggs from rolling away. It will also keep the birds and their eggs off the wet ground. Often there are thousands of nests in a rookery.

After about three days the female or mother penguins return. There are thousands of males already

Above: When courting, the male and female
 chinstraps perform for each
 other. Penguins mate with
 the same partner year after
 year.
Left: Gentoo penguin lays its eggs
 on a pebble nest.

in the rookery. The females
look for last year's mates.
They find each other by
sounds they make. The
mating pairs bow and
stretch their necks upward
and make loud noises.

Thousands of young Adélie penguins are born each year.

Now both birds bring pebbles to the nest. Several days after they mate, the female lays one greenish-white egg. Within three days she lays a second egg.

It has been about three weeks since the mother penguin last ate. Now she goes to the sea to feed.

The father Adélie keeps the eggs warm for more than two weeks. Every penguin has a brood patch of bare skin on its belly. The feathers spread apart to open the brood patch.

By the time the female returns, the male will have gone without eating for five to six weeks.

Now the female cares for the eggs. The hungry male heads for the sea. He is gone for two weeks. When he returns both parents care for the eggs. Five weeks after they were laid, the eggs hatch.

What a harsh world these chicks enter! Cold winds sweep down over the rookery. Sometimes blizzards almost cover the adult birds. Fortunately the chicks have parents to care for them.

Adult Adélie feeds its young half-digested or regurgitated food.

FROM CHICK TO FLEDGLING

When the baby chicks hatch, they are covered with a soft gray down. They must be kept warm in their parent's brood patch. They poke their tiny heads out only to feed from their parent's beak.

The tiny chicks must be fed small amounts of food very often. The parents take turns going down to the sea for fish, krill, or squid. The chicks reach up to their parent's beak to feed.

When the Adélie chicks are about ten days old, thicker brown feathers begin to push out the soft down. This is the first molt. With the heavier coat,

Close-up of Adélie penguins

three-week-old chicks can
leave the nest. Chicks
gather together in groups.

The fast-growing chicks
are always hungry. Now
both parents must catch
food. The chicks are

Unemployed adults watch over the young penguins.

guarded by "unemployed" adults. Sometimes they are birds who have lost a mate or their own chicks. It is their job to chase away the hunting birds. Guarding the babies is important work.

For four more weeks, the
parents feed the chicks.
The parents feed only their
own chicks.

Soon the chicks molt
again. They are juveniles
now. The fluffy brown
feathers are pushed out by
black and white feathers.

Molting Adélie
juvenile

At last when they are about seven weeks old the Adélies have complete shiny, waterproof suits. They learn to take oil from a special gland near the base of their tail. When they preen they spread this oil over their feathers with their beaks.

Now it is time for the young Adélies to feed themselves. When they feed themselves they are said to "fledge."

Molting gentoos stand in the warn sun.
It takes two or three weeks for a penguin
to grow a new suit of feathers.

The parents have worked very hard feeding their young. Their own feathers are badly worn. They are no longer a shiny black and white.

It will take two to three weeks to molt and grow a new suit of feathers. Once again the parents cannot eat. While they molt they have no protection from the icy cold water. Finally they are ready for the long swim northward.

The busy, noisy rookery is empty. Perhaps there were as many as 50,000 adults during the breeding season. But for almost seven months the rookery will be deserted. Next spring the cycle will start all over.

Chinstrap penguins

The same nesting
activities are followed by
other kinds of penguins,
especially the other two
brush-tails—the gentoo and
the chinstrap.

The gentoos are a little
larger than the Adélies.

Above: Gentoo juveniles
Right: Penguins nest in the
tussock grass on New
Island, one of the
Falkland Islands, off the
coast of Argentina.

Although gentoos nest near
Adélies, they can also be
found in warmer places.
There they may nest in the
tall, tussock grass.

Gentoo chicks look like
small copies of their

parents. They just lack the black throat and white flash over each eye and across the head. They fledge between two and three months after hatching.

The chinstraps are always willing to fight for their territory. They are called chinstraps because of the black band of feathers that runs down from their black heads under their chins.

Right: Chinstrap rookery on Nelson Island
Below: Humboldt penguins in a zoo

Chinstraps often have their rookeries far up a mountainside. They may have to pass close to Adélies or gentoos to reach their own nests. They come ashore after the Adélies have selected the best sites.

Penguin watching in a zoo or marine park is almost as much fun as seeing them in their rookeries. Penguins are truly amazing birds.

WORDS YOU SHOULD KNOW

antarctic(ant • ARK • tick)—about or in the region around the
South Pole

brood patch—an area of bare skin on the penguin's belly where
the eggs and young penguins are kept to stay warm

burrow(BER • oh)—a hole, tunnel, or opening dug in the ground by
a small animal

colony(KAHL • ah • nee)—a group of the same kind of animals
living together

defense(dih • FENCE)—to protect from attack or harm; to guard

desert(dih • ZERT)—to leave; abandon

equator(ee • KWAIT • er)—the imaginery line that goes around the
middle of the earth halfway between the North and South
Poles

fledge(FLEJ)—the time when the young penguin is ready to take
care of itself

harsh—rough and unpleasant

krill—small shrimp like animals that live in the ocean and are used
as food by other animals

lack—to not have; absence

mate(MAIT)—to pair; to join together to have young

molt(MOHLT)—to shed

preen—in birds to dress the feathers with oil using the beak

regurgitate(ree • GERJ • ih • tait)—in birds, to bring up partly
digested food from the stomach so it can be fed to the
young birds

rookery(ROOK • er • ee)—an area where birds gather to mate and
give birth to young

tussock grass(TUSS • uck GRASS)—a kind of grass that grows
in clumps

INDEX

About the Author

Emilie Utteg Lepthien earned a BS and MA Degree and certificate in school administration from Northwestern University. She taught third grade, upper grade science and social studies, was a supervisor and principal of Wicker Park School for twenty years. Mrs. Lepthien has also written and narrated science and social studies scripts for the Radio Council (WBEZ) of the Chicago Board of Education.

Mrs. Lepthien was awarded the American Educator's Medal by Freedoms Foundation. She is a member of Delta Kappa Gamma Society International, Illinois Women's Press Association, National Federation of Press Women, Iota Sigma Epsilon Journalism sorority, Chicago Principals Association, and active in church work. She has co-authored primary social studies books for Rand, McNally and Company and served as educational consultant for Encyclopaedia Britannica Films. She is the author of Australia *in the Enchantment of the World series published by Childrens Press. She has traveled to all seven continents including two visits to Antarctica where she found the penguins especially interesting.*